Second Edition

Publisher: Powered by Above
Author: Deborah Tant
Photography: dreamstime–www.dreamstime.com
and Deborah Tant

Paperback ISBN: 978-0-6458116-2-9
Hardback ISBN: 978-0-645811-9-8
E-book ISBN: 978-0-6458116-3-6

www.poweredbyabove.com
Poweredbyabove@poweredbyabove.com

DEDICATION

To planet Earth.
Thank you for sharing your beauty every single day.

Snowball is a young humpback whale who loves to have fun
flipping and slapping his fins and his tale with his bum.
He loves the winter sun while he journeys up the east coast
by showing off how big he can splash and loves to boast.

It is a very long journey from Antarctica
to the North Queensland Coast of Australia.

19,000km or 12,000 miles,

it's a long distance but Snowball always smiles.

He and his pod friends have loads of fun along the way,

including singing beautiful songs,

that travel great distances and linger all day.

Along the journey they make lots of new friends,

dolphins, seals, turtles and penguins.

They teach each other new tricks and places to go

like beaches, reefs, coral ledges and blow holes.

The round trip takes 265 days,

which is a very long time and they should be praised.

For their long trip, they eat up big,

for several days they get as fat as a Pig.

They eat up to 1.5 tons of krill a day,

to keep them going on their traveling way.

When they travel, they fast, don't eat at all

and live off their body fat

while they holiday and have a ball.

Male humpback whales are famous for singing loud and proud,

they sing beautiful songs to a very big crowd.

They sing to all the creatures in the sea,

and can be heard for 24 hours, can you believe?

Their singing can be heard a long distance away

up to 185 kms or 115 miles while they play.

Do you know how the humpback whale

looks out of the water?

They are very cleaver with three ways of

of checking everything is in order.

They can blow water,

they can spy hop

and

they can breech their large bodies.

When they blow water.

They blow water out of their blow hole,

high into the sky as they play and roll.

The blow holes act like our noses,

to help them breath while they do their poses.

When they spy hop.

They pop out of the water vertically and strong,

to take a look at who is out there

and if his friends are coming along.

When they breech.

They dive out of the water vertically and high,

with most of their bodies going up to the sky.

They throw themselves onto their backs or on their sides,

then back into the water to play and hide.

Do you know how fast Snowball can

travel during the migration?

When he is generally cruising,

it is about 7 km or 4.3 mph that he is moving.

But when they are playing and chasing,

it is 18km or 11 mph and he is racing.

Snowball's migration starts off in Antarctica,

with the summer feeding grounds being their starter.

The long journey takes them to Eden and Twofold Bay,

where you can watch thousands of whales leading the way.

They continue up the coast,

passing through Byron Bay and the Gold Coast.

Then on to Morton and Hervey Bay,

where they reach the magnificent Great Barrier Reef

and sing hooray!

Finally, they arrive at Cairns which is their destination,

where it is time to turn around near the basin.

Now on their way home through the Great Barrier Reef,

this now becomes their winter calving grounds,

although ever so brief.

They continue along down to the
Gold Coast and then Byron Bay.
This is now the nursing and resting grounds
for babes and mothers without delay.

It is time for Snowball to make his

way home to the South Pole,

where the Antarctic waters could chill your soul.

Back to a diet of krill, shrimp and fish,

the essential food source for Snowball, delish.

You can see they have long strands of Baleen,

that are long and fibrous and never green.

Baleen they have instead of teeth,

it gives them a big smile when they greet and meet.

The Baleen is really there to sieve and help them eat,

to keep them well and healthy as they don't eat meat.

Facts About Snowball.

Whales don't sleep – did you know that?

They can switch off half of their brain to rest
while the other half is focused on breathing, bless.

Humpback whales live on average 50 years,
and when they pass, humpback whales
are know to grieve with tears.
There have been rare cases of individuals living,
longer than usual, to 100 years, no kidding.

It is time for Snowball and his friends to say

Good-bye

Until next time

A Small Favor to Ask...

Now that you have come to the end of my book,
what did you think of Snowball's story?
It would mean the world to me if you could leave an
honest review on Amazon.

Thank you for your support. 🧡

The links to the review pages are below,
once there you will need to scroll down
a few pages to find the Review Option.

If you live in the **US** the link is:
www.amazon.com/dp/0645811629

If you live in the **UK** the link is:
www.amazon.co.uk/dp/0645811629

If you live in the **DE** the link is:
www.amazon.com.de/dp/0645811629

If you live in the **FR** the link is:
www.amazon.com.fr/dp/0645811629

If you live in the **IT** the link is:
www.amazon.com.it/dp/0645811629

If you live in the **ES** the link is:
www.amazon.com.es/dp/0645811629

If you live in the **CA** the link is:
www.amazon.com.ca/dp/0645811629

If you live in **AU** the link is:
www.amazon.com.au/dp/06545811629

www.ingramcontent.com/pod-product-compliance
Lightning Source LLC
Chambersburg PA
CBHW042018090426

42811CB00015B/1676